MW00610240

The Animals
of
My Earth School

Also by Mildred Kiconco Barya

Give Me Room to Move My Feet
The Price of Memory after the Tsunami
Men Love Chocolates But They Don't Say

The Animals
of
My Earth School

For Ruthie,
Wishing you a lovely creature life

Mildred Kiconco Barya

Terrapin Books

Terrapin Books
4 Midvale Avenue
West Caldwell, NJ 07006

www.terrapinbooks.com

ISBN: 978-1-947896-63-5
Library of Congress Control Number: 2022950490

First Edition

Cover art: Rosanna Tasker
www.rosannatasker.com
Animals of My Earth School
Mixed Media illustration using gouache paint, wax pastel, and
watercolour pencil
30 x 40 inches

Cover design: Diane Lockward

for Woodsy, my favorite animal in the world

Contents

Every beetle is a gazelle in the eyes of its mother.

—African proverb

Insecta

Giant Stag Beetles

Friends of dead wood and seclusion,
to know you is to go underground.

It is not known why you sing in your larval form
by rubbing parts of your body together.

Perhaps that's how you speak your presence to your kind.
So you stridulate and give off sounds and eat ginger—

a spiced life, a long childhood
before pupating and finding a new seduction—lights.

The moment you emerge you're ready to copulate.
You've spent up to six years buried under, why waste time?

Though I have seen snakes shedding skin,
never your kind discarding outer layers.

You remain a mystery even as you bare yourself to the light.
As soon as you enter new life among the woodlands, you're gone.

Coccinellidae

With their cute red bodies speckled with black dots,
ladybugs are welcomed into my house, bed, and hair.
I become aware of their presence when my feet touch the floor.
When I turn on the lights. When I run fingers through my hair.

I don't see their wings until they're in flight. One is
climbing my white kitchen sink and skirts the edges
with a confidence that astounds me. As if this is her
familiar territory, after all. And I, the stranger.

For some reason, the bug reminds me of my ex. Small head
and tiny legs dragging along a large body. I could squash it
between my thumb and index finger. The thought doesn't
startle me. I recognize it in the same manner that a mug of hot

coffee holds the capacity to cause damage, and yellow jackets
on my favorite trail probably entertain similar thoughts.
Perhaps, it's the recognition, rather than mere
compassion, that prevents any one of us from testing our limits.

Let it seep out. Feel spacious. What if I swallow the beetle? As I
lean closer, she senses me—retracts her legs inside her body like
a turtle. Stops all movement and commands me to be still as well.
Outdoors later, in the presence of a male, her back opens, lifts

and welcomes the sexual juices pumped into her. Then, with an equally roaring appetite, she gives in to another hunger—skips from one squash leaf to the next, gorging on aphids and pests— an attribute that endears her to the farmers. They call her God's

little cow. Easily kills and consumes. When I surrender my heart to her, I wonder if she prefers walking to flying, as if it matters.

Music

When cicadas sing
do they know
I am listening

to the silence of
what could become
the future?

A world without Joy
marking the end of
underground movement.

Their name—fulfilled
their bodies *cut up*
beyond what science
initially conceived.

The Anthropocene
has adopted satiation
strategies to overwhelm
their senses.

Their emergence
preceded humans.
Generous choir
lost on us.

The World Is Necessary, Even for Little Ants

Digging mounds between
a grove of pine, carrying piles
of food larger than themselves,
stocking up for winter. Do humans
have the means to live differently?

When my phone vibrates, a shot
of long lines at food banks, not unlike
the ones before me, is followed by my
lover's text—would you believe thousands
of hungry civilians waiting for hours—

My God, hard times! Nation crumbles
At my feet. Jaws open. Lord,
grant us mercy, even if in small
doses. Let us feed   clothe   and
house all in need.

Let us not be known as the people
who withhold compassion instead
of serving the greater good.
I want to see goodness for you,
for me, for all of us living creatures.

In my old country ants will strip a forest
bare. Whatever it takes   patience grows
hard work   hard times, tireless labors—
oh, how they travail—community-minded.
Let us be   come   ants   to one another.

Locusts

In the year of the locust invasion, people ate barks. It was all they could find. The rest of the plants and gardens were bare. Women chased after the locusts with pans, but a stranger appeared and warned them not to eat any. Then he left. Meanwhile people were starving and the barks were mostly bitter.

The first man to die lost his mind, and the second, and third. The first ran around his yard naked, and the children cried, *Ayee.*

The stranger returned holding entrails in his hands and said since they had not obeyed his word, everyone would die. He advised them to hurry to the coffin maker so that when death struck, they'd be ready, waiting in their coffins. He suggested that they get a griot to write tomb inscriptions for future generations to know how their ancestors had fared.

For two days the coffin maker was the happiest person. He had never made so much money! He whistled as he worked and built everyone the kind of coffin they wanted, using expensive plywood, mahogany, ebony, mature oak . . . For expedited service, he charged exorbitant prices.

On the third day, people started to get into their coffins. To his horror, the coffin maker was the first to feel a fever, followed by a chill that made his spine tingle like a caterpillar dancing. Acute pain colonized his neck and temples, and a numbing heaviness fogged his brain while severe cramps attacked his joints, shoulders, and muscles. He realized he wouldn't have any use for the money, and he hadn't even made for himself a marvelous coffin.

Who Loves Mosquitoes?

Mosquitoes bug us.
They assault our bodies
and sneak into our beds
in a boarding house in Jamaica.

We spray lavender
and crush them in our palms.
The more we kill, the more
attack us. In Nature,

the game of survival is won
by those who outnumber their
enemies. We're no match.
It's our first night. Our host

hears us slapping walls
and apologizes. Then she says,
The next couple of days will be
worse with the muggy weather.

Heads Are Unnecessary for Copulation

The revered insect devours her skinny husband with delight.
First, they make love. At the critical moment, she bites off
his head. I stand in awe of this cannibalistic mantis.
How many husbands will she consume before she meets
her own predator? Her green coat in the bushes hides her
well just like the ghost family finds protection among trunks
and leaves that match their brown hues. I mistake
the brightly colored for flowers.

While taking a passport photograph some time ago, I was told
that I move my whole body like an insect—instead of just
the head. But not the mantises. After numerous attempts to pose
upright, I still had a missing ear and the right shoulder raised
several degrees above the left. My failure at precision makes me
admire the prophets—in Greek. Also known as Hottentot gods
in Southern Africa. They can turn their small triangular
heads to perfectly knowing, intelligent looks. With five eyes
their wisdom compound, and when night comes, the light
in their vision changes colors.

Imagine what humans could do with such stimuli and perception
of depth. Like old gods, they're always hungry, fierce,
and bloodthirsty. Crossing from praying to preying
when they find a willing sacrifice.

Skilled stalkers of the hunt, they move with a sensuous slink,
only to rapidly grab and trap their good catch between spiked
raptorial legs faster than I can blink. Soothing caresses ensue—

pecking, rubbing, sucking, pinching, nibbling, and rocking
back and forth. Then ripping apart. Devoted foreplay
purposed to charm and tenderize the lover coming
to pieces and swallowed with gusto like we do.

Mammalia I

Creation

I wish for myself
the god Mercury's
speed and lightness
as I create. But what
appears through my
door is a methodical
hedgehog.

Timid ugly body
covered with spikes
and stiff to the touch,
sits by my side,
anointed.

Much as I try to
ignore it, I grow
fond of its ways—
its punctilious
nature roots in me.

We work quietly
through the night,
sharing secrets,
curiosity born
out of containment
and clear focus.

In my longings
I've sought airborne

symbols instead of
paying attention to
what's noticing me
by the hedge. Oh,
the gift of clarity!

Mercury shows up
occasionally, but if I'm
to remember one thing,
and one thing only, it's
my hedgehog's staying
power that sustains.

Moon Dog

She
Wolf lifts her sleek head and wails into the full moon.
Stresses of her life—
elevated cortisol levels
attributed to human presence.

The moon halts to absorb her anguish.
Wolf's face glows and feels very beautiful.

By the time she leaves the cliff's edge, her heart
is filled with gladness and renewed confidence

to lay the foundations of a great city,
with her breast milk.

He
Wolf sees his powerful muscled shadow in
the moonlight and falls in love. He adores
and woos the moon with his gut-spilling laugh.
Pledges devotion—expressions of affection
across great distance. To hunt and to hold,
to mate forever—*till death do us part.*

The moon smiles coquettishly. Wolf
brings wildflowers and, another time,
a jar of moonshine. The moon giggles
and says, *Silly Wolf! Don't you see I
already got my shine?* Wolf gets angry

that he's mocked, and his respect for the
moon evaporates. He bares his fangs close
to the moon's face, and the moon withdraws.

Journey of the Lone Wolf to Sirius
I am coming home to the gods,
but how lonely the moon traveling alone.

Where is the Dog Star? Is it visible only for her?
How I envy the moon her secret company.

My desire for companionship contradicts
my fear of others, and punctures my solitude

with tension. How sorrowful the moon as she
listens to my woes, capable witness to what

I feel. How lovely we must be together.
How indulgent and so complete.

Wolf's Call for the Wolf People
Dear Wolf,
How like God, sinewed with complexity.
Loved, abhorred, heavily mythologized.
We would create you if you didn't exist.
You take the medal for monogamous affairs.
We can never fully understand you.

Everything human and animal vibrates in you:
violence, intelligence, hot sex, insatiable appetite—
always hungry! Your growls and whines

have animated our psyches from the time
the world began, ancient and modern.

When you howl into the moon's belly,
timbre across the hills and valleys causes our
tired bones to rise. To pick up hoes, hunting
bows, and carpentry tools. Knowing too well
our primal fears, and bringing us renewal.

City of Antelope

The antelope is missing
from the national air.
There's a flag instead with a
crested crane in a white disk.

Citizens want to know:
Where is the impala that
gave the city its name when
the first plunderers asked,
What place is this,
hilly and full of impala?

The city continues to morph into
more cities splitting and sprawling
beyond the seven hills.

Dictators and liberators dream
the city into new memories
and abandon the ones they grew up
with. They create new pasts into
presents that the future can
contain. What happens should
the city run out of space?

Time to time, political wars plunge
the city into chaos. Blood flows in
the rivers, valleys, and alleyways
where the people once danced and

made love. Burned and destroyed,
emptiness and ugliness seize control.
Those who do not die flee, crying,
We cannot recognize the city!

Fresh dreams rebuild the city with hope
and bricks and vibrant colors. Suburbs
previously separate from the former city
become part of the renovated city and
swallow up minor cities within the city.

It's the nature of dreams to alter and
exclude, reject and exaggerate certain
features in the struggle to remodel
new shapes and designs. Nowadays,
the city's futility is a blueprint based
on tourists' likes and impressions.

Someday, there will be another
imagined city burgeoning from the
placenta like years on a tree trunk. But
the freedom fighter whose limb was
amputated will see a stump braced with
a substitute pushing in and out of strides.

Ode to the Sheep

after Yusef Komunyakaa's "Ode to a Drum"

Sheep, I want to say,
for your sake
you'll make me beautiful,
but that's not true.
Rather, for my conscience.
The meat is great,
but that's not what
this is about. We kill
for texture—
to feel the other
beneath our feet.
I watch my father
ramming fists into you,
membrane tearing,
pushing against your
skin, until you're bare—
a glossy redness.
You're the son sacrificed
for a daughter. I want
to say, Thank you.
But your blood
collecting into the pan
stops me. I'll be sixteen,
is what I whisper
as I close your eyes.
You're in me,

I'm in you.
The party begins.
Compliments on my shoes,
give you back life.

The Heart, the Heart, the Hunger

I once had a blue wooden horse.
Maybe it was brown.
I carried the horse everywhere.
I slept with that horse,
fed it my love,
gave it all the love it could never return.

I called it Mother Horse and it broke me into
crimson speckled fragments, insect-like.
The smallest of hearts goes to the fairyfly.
It lays its eggs in the eggs
of other insects. Parasitic wasp.
You'd need a microscope to see its heart.
The human heart is like that sometimes.

Did you know that the Etruscan shrew
is the living mammal with the smallest heart?
It eats constantly—twice as much its
body weight to not starve to death.
I incline my ears to the little mammal.
1,200 to 1,500 heartbeats per minute.
How fragile, tender, and tough
Savi's pygmy shrew, white-toothed pygmy shrew,
carrying the weight of too many
names, too many beats, for a small heart.

In cremation, I am told, the heart is
the last organ to burn. Bit by bit.

Flight

There's a cat from time to time.
This spotted and golden Savannah

with massive ears was getting eye
injections, sticky tears burning its

cheeks. Claws trimmed, rendered
useless. Easy meal. I was floating—

that's the best part—flew over
traffic, golf courses, and terraced

hills. My lungs buoyant as I took
in the mountain air.

Guilted Tenderness

Mother cow gives birth to a small baby.
A few hours later the calf struggles to stand.

Mother licks it clean and moves her teats
closer, but it's ignorant of suckling.

A man in black work boots and faded blue
overalls brings a lump of moldy cheese,

perhaps to trigger its sense of smell,
but the calf declines to eat. Then

the man pushes into its mouth what looks
like breadcrumbs. Still, the calf won't feed.

A rush of compassion washes over me. We
were all once like that, newly born and helpless.

Some babies instinctively know how to suckle.
Others have to be nudged. I walk away feeling

tender, wishing for the calf to grow strong as
we drink the milk and replenish with colostrum.

The Lost Bull

I'm at Zach's home, my childhood friend,
looking for my family's bull which has
strayed. Zach's mother has just harvested
sweet potatoes with purple skin. Their valley
is bursting with abundance—mangoes,
avocados, oranges, and wild blackberries.

I'm afraid we might be fined a hefty sum if the
bull eats or destroys what belongs to our neighbors.
My father will be wasp-mad since he'd asked me
to take care of it. I must have dozed off. There I
was lying on my back in the tall elephant grass,
my eyes arrested by the bluest sky I've ever seen.

Once or twice, I glanced at the bull. Two white
egrets perched on its back catching insects, the bull
contentedly chewing cud. Next thing I knew—
no bull and no egrets. I tell all this to Zach while
he rolls for me a delicious chapati stuffed with fried
rice and meat, red onions, peppers, and tomatoes.

After I've eaten, Zach escorts me home. On our way
he asks that I keep quiet when we arrive. He'll flip the
story—my life in jeopardy when the bull charged at me.
I had to escape. Probable. As I picture myself trampled
and gored by the bull, I shake with laughter. My
apprehension lifts. Off we go to face my dad.

The Human-headed Lion Seduces
Three Lambs

We are roasting a chunk of tenderloin beef by the roadside—my older brother, my younger sister, and someone who looks like David from my high school. He laughs like David and talks like David. He's supposed to be telling us stories. He says he has good ghost stories.

Where we are is new to me. I do not remember living or moving here, yet I own the orange apartment across the road. Other than a few shrubs and scanty dwarf trees, the ground is covered with loose white sand and concrete. We're in a city but what city? Why aren't we in a park or some other picnic-friendly place?

A few meters from our barbecue, we see a lion with a human head enticing three lambs. The lion tells them that he knows a field of green pasture where they can feed to their fullest. He sticks out his tongue and slowly licks his mouth—cute and disturbing all at once. I expect the lambs to flee, but they begin fidgeting, scratching the ground with their cloven hooves. The lion steps forward—closing the distance between—and grins. The lambs gaze at the lion's face. Have you ever looked into the dilated pupils of a lion's eyes? They're filled with peace and light. Ambered appetite. Persuasion. The lambs enter the land of believability and walk with the lion. We know he's going to eat them; he wants to fatten them for his own good.

What is it in the realm of desire that elicits trust? Between the green and red traffic signs, what pushes pedestrians to ignore the solid amber light and cross the road? What urges cars to drive past a flashing yellow strobe?

The sweet and pungent smell of smoked chilies, onions, and garlic flavors the air. I gather some sticks to beat the lion in case he comes back for us. If I close my eyes and listen deeply, I can hear the lowered pitch and muted resonance in the lion's voice. Seeking obedience and worst of all—sacrifice. Perhaps none of us can resist a lion clothed in a language that appeals to our senses. The lion works his magic, his golden eyes flecked with charm.

Aves

Falling in Love

A procession of wild turkeys delights me.
I watch them pause by my red automobile

and take turns at the reflectors.
They've discovered their own beauty,

a fascinating thing to behold. I'm shameless to say
I look forward to seeing them daily. I've rearranged

my tasks and routines to be home early when eleven turkeys
emerge from the woods. They remind me of my youth

growing up in a home without mirrors. Once in a while, I'd go
with my sisters to the bathroom of a guest house to do our makeup

in front of its large mirror. When we became adults,
we bought pocket-size mirrors that fit in our purses.

I've never bothered to ask why we didn't have any in the house.
Maybe there were more important things on our parents' minds than

looking at one's reflection. When I bought the vehicle, it was love—
visualizing myself transported to places of wonder. I had not

imagined that the wild turkeys too would be charmed to see
themselves in the mirrors of my car and fall in love.

Will There Be Chickens in Paradise?

A bearded stranger puts a crystal ball into my hands.
There's a chick inside, a few days to hatching.

Its skinny body is diaphanous white and it moves—
muscles, tissues, organs—a faint, beating heart
inside a thin membrane of amniotic fluid.

I squeeze the ball lightly and my heart skips a beat.
Cluck-cluck. I close my eyes and see the image of
Lot's wife, eyes petrified. The ground opens and traps
her body in a pillar of white and pink Himalayan salt
rising from her feet all the way to the top of her head
like a shroud. As it thickens, a few particles fall back
and form a foundation where her feet had been.

I do not understand what this image has to do with me
or the chick, which I believe is innocent in all this.

I find myself thinking about Paradise,
wishing that chickens would be in it.

Bewilderment

I'm sitting with a laptop at the dining table in my living room.
The backyard door is open, ruffled leaves sway in the breeze.
A hummingbird flies in, pecks my cheek with zest, and buzzes out.
I am astonished and relieved it's not smacked my eye instead.

An echo of its sound settles in my ears. How loud it bumbles
for a bird that weighs less than a nickel! Quivers like a strong
locomotive—the force of a hummer. Yes, the name makes sense.
A world of iridescent colors floods my vision—bright reds,
yellows, and deep greens. Royal purple stripes fit for a king.

Disneyland's magic cannot compare in visuals and acoustics
with the splendid pomp and vanishing of the hummingbird.
Everything around me is changed. Even when I look
at the refrigerator, stove, and pans, all shimmer.

Sword-billed hummingbird, what you love opens to your
sharp beak—esperanza, hibiscus, morning glory, nasturtium,
and my heart—penetrated, wells with unspeakable joy.
A new burst of energy almost knocks me off the chair.
I want to name you sugar bird, but it's taken.

Ruler of the South, the Aztec god of war chose your form.
Speak to me of your propensity for work and net benefits,
of intimacy and how to sustain a long-distance relationship—
a 500-mile nonstop flight across the water—fueled by
passion, reaching for nectar and awake to my own mysteries.

Little Wren

We speak our hope to see you in flight.
Grandma says, Hope has no place
where conditions are sunshine.

She thrives amidst sorrow and grief,
drags her tired feet to a resting nest and
protects our timid hearts with armadillo vests.

She summons your courage that rouses
our great spirits to dream big and follow
you from the Old World to the New.

Bold in ambition, you fancied a crown,
perched on an eagle's tail and flew to the
summit to be elected the King of Birds.

When the eagle approached the throne,
how loud you sang and shook for all to see
you'd won. Long before we had surgeons,

your precision kept you alive as you probed
into crevices for grub with your slender
bill. I love your appetite and belligerence

when it suits you. Your voice reminds me
of my old Volvo in winter. Raw and
scratchy, but it never fails to start.

With you, Grandma has a mouth of bellows
fanning flames for wounded wings to
persist and fight until we get home.

Eggs

I'm with a friend who
might be my new boyfriend.

We watch a hen lay three large eggs
in a mound of dust. My friend decides

we should help the hen and carry its eggs to
our home to prevent them from getting eaten

by other creatures. He picks up the eggs and the
hen follows closely. I rejoice in its cooperation.

It has red earlobes and brown eggs whose
whites I imagine firm and free from defects.

We'll put it in a little hen house where it can
safely lay more eggs and hatch them.

On our way we stop to buy grapefruit, bittersweet
in the late light of our walk's end. Then the first

crack—what came first? An argument. Perplexing.
Isn't potentiality always in existence long before

anything concrete can manifest? Prior to coming
across the chicken, everything looked promising—

Grade A. When we arrive at our door, teeth on edge,
we taste beyond question what we have become.

Why I Wake Up Early

I have eleven wild turkeys that play
and dance and eat all day. Tiny heads,
wrinkly necks, and at ease in their
seemingly awkward bodies! I doubt they
ever suffer from low self-esteem. Males
prance around the females with pride, fanning
their tails and flaunting all they've got—
fleshy blue and red wattles. They are royals.

Soon there will be turkey babies who will
learn the daily walks and rituals of their
parents. They all pass by my red door
without knocking, but I hear them all the
same—their cackle and, holy gods! how I
envy their agility even when they are plump!
Oh, the joy they bring me as I watch them
so free. Do they have any cares, or is this

what it means to belong to the Universe?
I rise to greet them each day. My heart
pounds with concern when I do not see them
at the expected time. I imagine the worst—
bears, foxes, humans . . . but before I can go
on with my wretched thoughts, they show up.
I do not wait for another sign to assure me
that I, too, am loved somehow.

Dazzling Wickedness

One summer at a beach in Northern California, a raven stalked me. It was determined to have my tomato and cheese sandwich. Farther up the shore was a large, vaulted rock that I ran to. Before crawling inside, I turned and surveyed the coast, saw no raven in pursuit, then sat down. I enjoyed the breeze coming through the entrance and cooling my face. Just as I relaxed and took a bite into the juicy sandwich, the raven sprang into the space between my outstretched feet and eyeballed me. My tummy clenched in terror. What speed possessed me! I tore the sandwich and threw a chunk outside. *Do not feed the animals.* No, oh, no. Concern for the raven's agency to fend for itself was nowhere near the charge for my safety. I could have lost an eye! The raven glared at what remained in my hand. Jesus! I tossed that too, and lastly the backpack. The raven, I swear to God, tiptoed around me as if to make sure I wasn't hiding anything else, then spun violently and flew outside. Its unkindness so confounded me that long after I'd left the beach, I remained tormented by the dazzling wickedness of its powerful gaze.

How Can It Be a Cardinal Sin?

Iron sharpens iron. And like attracts like in diverse forms. That cardinal over there in the rhododendron hedgerow is in love with a robin. I witnessed their courtship while sipping Earl Grey tea on my porch. The way to the robin's heart is through her belly. The cardinal brings berries and sunflower seeds to feed her, beak-to-beak. Are they the only birds in the yard? No, yet they've found each other.

Kiss kiss kiss, he sweetly whistles. Amused, perhaps, she tries him. *Wait wait wait*, he sings louder like clear wind chimes. *Whoit whoit whoit*, his throat warbles. And one more time he rings her bells: *Tuututututututu*.

She appears to smack him but plants a kiss on his head.

Now they're frolicking and nesting together.

Relentless Play: The Nature of Struggle

One morning, I am witness to a confrontation
between a young owl and four crows. The first crow
is on the ground picking insects in my front yard, or so
it seems. Later I discover that its job is operational—
like a cartographer mapping out the area of struggle.

(The other three crows are tormenting a baby
owl in the pine tree behind my house).

The ground control crow caws and the others
respond raucously to the battle call. Then it
flies to the tree and joins the murder.

The owl jumps to a lower branch, and the crows
redistribute themselves to form a ring around it.
One crow darts onto the owl's branch, while the
rest cry feverishly. The owl spreads its wings,
raises its head, and in that moment looks bigger,
but one can still tell it's not a full-grown bird.
It arches towards the taunting crow, heads almost
touching. I'm not sure if there's fear in either bird's
eyes or sheer determination. Which will win?

Eventually, the owl skips to another tree and
all the crows chase after it. Where's the
parliament of owls to defend the young?
Is this how our children will be betrayed?

The birds continue to harass and provoke each other, springing from tree to tree, branch to branch, each expecting perhaps that the other will strike first, open the fight. When the owl finally gets to the tree in my front yard, the crows leave it alone. That's how I realize that the ground crow, a leader of sorts, had outlined the circumference of the struggle.

In my quiet, I've wondered if the birds had really intended to fight or, were they simply testing each other's endurance and will?

It's dawned on me that while there's struggle in the nature of all that exists, there's also unmistakable fluid grace, skill, and bold engagement. Heated tension, yes. But in my human relations, under similar pressure, do I hold myself back in honor of something greater, like dignity? Haven't the birds demonstrated that their existence—like their struggle—isn't about insult or assault but relentless play—albeit frenzied?

When the call comes for me, I pray to remember the owl and squawking crows.

Effects of the White Parrot Fairy Tale

After reading the White Parrot fairy tale, a small-size parrot appears in my dream and pokes my right temple, then sinks its beak deeper. I look to one of my siblings sitting in the garden to help, but he's stoned. Can't even see me. I must extract the parrot myself but not when it's awake. I must endure the longest wait of my life. Until this moment everything came to me easily. I'm on a new mission now. Eventually, the commotion subsides. The parrot falls asleep. I clench my fingers around its body and start pulling. As soon as I have it in my hands, all the stones in the garden come to life. But before we can all celebrate, I run to the bathroom to wash the gaping wound with hydrogen peroxide.

Reptilia

The Graceful Alligator

Every day at 7:15 a.m., the alligator glides gracefully past our home
by the canal. We watch from the bank as it moves in a straight line,
joyful to see it once more, to anticipate its comings and goings.

I marvel at its perfect symmetry and internalized chronometer—
I struggle with routine and understanding my body's relation to space.
If you tell me to jump into a swimming pool straight up and down,
I'll bend my body in motion and won't even know it.
Those watching ask, Is there a glitch between my brain's coordination
and the nervous system?

I want to argue that non-linearity has a place, but I keep quiet.
I'm told most people can bounce upright. Most people can steer
a kayak uniformly in one direction. Most people can swim
with grace like the alligator.

I've concluded my joints and muscles don't connect at points of grace.
Does that indicate disgrace? I ignore the advice to seek a diagnosis
of my affliction. I feel fine. I forget which:
　　　What you don't know can't hurt you;
　　　What you don't know can kill you.
Like the alligator trusting poisoned water.

Factors

Lizards will on purpose sever their tails when in stressful or dangerous situations, an act known as *autotomy*—from the Greek auto "self" and tome "severing" or self-amputation. Even after the tail is cast off, it goes on wriggling, hence distracting the lizard's attacker. The lizard can regenerate its tail in a few weeks. The new tail will contain cartilage rather than bone and vary distinctly, not only in color but in texture, compared to its earlier appearance. In humans, change in skin pigment and texture are due to disease, rather than protective behavior. I heard of a South African woman who was once white but turned black over time. It wasn't the reptile genes calling, but a condition known as hyperpigmentation. Her husband asked for a divorce and took off with their three children.

The only mammals that come close to regeneration are the African spiny mice. Upon capture, they release their skin. Imagine a predator holding its prey only to realize seconds later that it has escaped, leaving only its skin. The mice regrow their skin, hair follicles, glands, fur, and cartilage with little or no scarring. Organic surgery at its finest.

Empirical sources suggest, "Lizards whose tail is a major storage organ for accumulating reserves, will return to a discarded tail after the threat has passed and eat it to recover the supplies." This makes me think that when we discarded our tails as Homo sapiens, we were supposed to swallow them in order to keep our reserves intact. We forgot a significant part of ritual and opened ourselves to disease, predators, and a weaker immune system.

Strangely, while looking in the mirror, I notice some things have fallen off my body and I can't locate them on the floor. Others attach to me like textile fabrics in all the wrong places. They fracture my ego, and I must find consolation that these zones of weakness make me softer.

I want to know more about the self-amputation act, free will and all, but the English dictionary corrects the word to autonomy: self-rule, independence, freedom, sovereignty, which surprisingly concern the lizards when they're shedding tails; compelled by their strong desire to remain free, safe, uneaten, untrapped, unconquerable, and not subdued in accordance with their survival manual.

Don't Bite the Hand That Feeds You

I'm cutting grass with a sickle
in the big yard where I once spent
my childhood running.

Iridescent snakes spit and pee
to soften the grass for me.
Flashes of white light emanate

from forked tongues,
and a fragrance like rose water,
like fresh spring swells above.

When the sharp blade of my
sickle catches their bodies' glint,
I blink, blinded by the radiance

and dancing fire in their eyes.
I'm kept warm in the serpentine
waves, circling back and forth,

honored that I'm chosen to be
in their company. My eyes mist
at this terrifying grace.

Mother comes out in her pink
nightgown to thank me. What time
is it? I ask. I'm anxious to get to school.

Eight o'clock, she says. Before I can
put away the sickle, Mother phones the
principal to say I'm assisting her.

She keeps me home and shows me a new
patch to mow. Too frightened to disobey,
I move over. The snakes glide ahead

with a confidence that comes from bellies aligned
with the beating heart of Earth, and in touch with
all the wisdom of the land unknown to my feet.

Dream of Lizard Solidarity

Out camping by myself
I'm transformed into
a bearded dragon.
A monitor lizard
flashes by with
a cheerful smile.

Then another and another
until there's a gathering—
lizards' intervention.
This is their territory.
Panic-stricken, I enter their
circle and beg for mercy.

They laugh and tell me
to take life less seriously.
It seems easy for them.
My throat, already
blackened by stress,
betrays me.

When I do not join
in their laughter,
they slither away.
I've disappointed
humans before.
Now, lizards.

A Jumping White Chameleon

Sparkling white and larger than most chameleons I've seen.
I'm afraid of its enormous eyes and stare, but I don't want it to get
injured. It's basking in the sun in the middle of a well-trodden path
near my house. Anyone and anything can trample on it.

I get hold of a long stick and approach the chameleon. My hope
is that it will see the stick, crawl, and coil around it. I'll lift the stick
gently with the chameleon on it and deposit it safely in the bush
farther down. However, as soon as it sees the stick, it leaps
right off the path. A marvel of a jump! Then it sings:

> You give me an inch,
> I take a foot.

Between the Dreaming and Becoming

Lizards are my friends, I tell the kid standing on the shoreline, one foot on a rock, a catapult in her hand, ready to throw pebbles in the water. Her orange overalls and red hair look wet. She could have risen from the sea, although her manner of ease makes me think she belongs here, on the surface of things.

She does not believe anything I say, but that's all right. I could get used to it.

One lizard opened up to me and said his name was Jacob. He does look like a Jacob if you know what I mean, the color of dark oak bearing acorns.

Jacob instructs me—how to walk on eggs covered with moss. A treacherous beauty. Step as if you're not stepping, as if slightly suspended in air, yet so close to the eggs. They couldn't be more slippery! I miss the humor and see danger instead. Of course, I fall. Yellow liquid running over green. I console myself: Who wouldn't? Jacob winks.

A woman who resembles my mother holds my hand, but I cannot trust her. My father appears, but I shake my head. Jacob asks, What do you really want?

As if he doesn't know—

Relax into play and laugh, laugh, laugh is what I want. Peel off the films, scales, blinds. Let me see clearly.

Dear Serpent

Your gaze depowers.

To break its hold,
we look away.

You fascinate your prey.
They cannot move.

How do we enter
your field
to disrupt
petrifying force
and exit on
a white horse
in golden light?

To stand in between
the third space—
the eye of a needle
intercepting magic,
the shield
reflecting back
horror to its kind.

Here's my wish:
I want to be
your friend,
carry *evil* for

the next fight
yet remain
pure at heart,
fluid in action,
no gap in mind
like a spark of
lightning fire.

Free but not
from immediate
attention.

I am an artist
looking at you.
Put the gaze
into this work—
bring out the
nature of art,
the way a fragile
egg hardens when
boiled, yet remains
soft inside.

Mammalia II

The Meat-loving God

How is tending sheep
preferred to tilling the land?

Two young farmers valued
their means of sustenance but
when time came to present
their gifts, one was favored
and the other cursed.

We are warned to not compare
apples with oranges, so I have no
business pitting broccoli against
the ram. But I do wonder how to
enjoy my work with a thankful
heart while awaiting criticism.

To you, oh Lord, I bring my choicest
fruit for blessing. Trained in the ancient
way, my labor in words I offer to you,
King of words. I, too, have avoided
blood except on a few pages. The smell
is horrible and makes me nauseous.

At home we worked the soil and kept
a flock. Our livestock consumed what
we did not use and grew fat grazing on
green grass, cabbage leaves, and carrots.
Turnips, parsnips, and potatoes were

tasty too. For animals to be worthy
of slaughter, they must eat greens
and fruit of the land. You and I are
sovereign in our choices. Your image
in me makes me like you. I am committed
to the tasks of my hands, head, and heart.

In the end, I admit, the jealous hand
wields the knife and slices the throat.
Anger management is rarely taught.
At what point did we turn you into
a monster? All those animals murdered
for you—lambs and bulls—ate
vegetables and grains. Cain and Abel—
your sacrifices too—have taught us
to judge harshly our offerings.

I have welcomed the fugitive nature of
all life—animals, plants, humankind—
everything I hold dear. I am told
the cockroaches will survive us all.

What's Not to Love?

The leopard comes
clothed in lust. Behold
his gaze, poised to pounce.

He wants her, it is clear.
But he'll wait in ambush—
anything—to come out on top.

He puts out his ruby tongue,
says he only eats vegetables. The red
stains on his teeth spring from a diet
of too many carrots and beetroot.

For his image, he wants so badly to be like
a yellow banana. Spotless. Squeezed for
ripeness. Peeled and ravished in large
mouthfuls. Oh pleasure. Oh mercy!

Just remember, a leopard is a leopard.
His nature cannot be repressed. He stalks,
crouches, and hunts all day. At night he
keeps vigil. Praise the depth of his prowess!

The god of wine and revelry donned
his print to bring on ecstasy.
Ashanti kings covered their stools
with his grandeur. No catwalk is complete

without a model in leotards
imitating his sensuous movements.

When the fading sunlight falls
on his tawny coat, he's raw
passion, elegant tail and whiskers,
the essence of soft fur and yearning.

Distinguished strategist. Ravenous.
He's all claws and rosettes, ready
to consume and make the elderly sigh.

The Shimmering Eyes of the Doe

This gentle animal's sound transcends puppy joy
atop the mountains and meadows where the brook

burbles along with her high-pitched seductive bleat.
She runs and jumps like a sunflower reaching for air, light,

and freedom to become everything that she is and will be.
I love her. Pure, crystal love. She knows she's ready, yet she

runs. Calls and controls the chase, strong muscles and
long limbs lifting off in liquid pleasure and grace.

God and Dog

Share the same
letters.

God writes to dog
about Elysian fields.

Dog wants to know if his
appetite would involve bones

even in Paradise.
Dog worries about a diet of greens,

but God pulls his tail and assures him,
Paradise belongs to those like him.

The Hyena

We pride ourselves on possessing reason—a faculty
believed to distinguish us from other animals as if
separation is a virtue, or the fact that this uniqueness
slows us down. To heart-think requires immediacy few
possess. *Mind like a Spark*—the way of the ancient warriors.
Like a hyena, the samurai instantly knew what to do
in the face of danger or pleasure. Eyes open. Swiftness
of action, no interval between tuning in or out.

But we are modern—we scroll through piles of experts'
spreadsheets to enlighten us to the pros and cons of alliances,
mortgages, Roth IRAs, traveling solo . . . We sift and sort until
we stagnate. Befuddled by a tangle of choices, the ego in the
way, we know too well the torturous state of indecision and
how to mask it with an intellectual haze that passes for
philosophical investigation. Without clarity, we discard
everything and start over—questioning thoughts and ideas as
they trickle through language—curbing the instinctual tongue.

To escape our fragmented and hollow selves, we dance naked.
Drink strong cocoa. Trade stories and eat mushrooms around
campfires of ceremonies that may return us to the laughing
hyena state in which we once knew all that we needed to know—
females come first. Patriarchy is dead. Nothing else matters.

In the kingdom of hyenas, the divine feminine reigns erect.
Adapts. Takes chances integrating feminine and masculine images,
guided by familial smells and sacred rituals. The hyena knows

her primal place in the system of things, untouched by slander and misgivings. Likewise, we must retrace our sharpness and wholeness not in science but in the sounds and silences of our drum circles. Leaving behind all doubt and misunderstandings.

For what it's worth, I am told we're all gifted in equal measure because Nature plays no favorites in the dominion of things.

The Dog Is Quiet

I want to dissolve
into a raindrop that
enters my mouth like
my lover's tongue,
aching hunger
swirling within,
bringing me to tears.

Suddenly, the radiator
comes on forcefully
ejecting heat. Outside,
pounding rain. The dog
that normally barks at
this hour is silent, as if
aware that this moment
does not need more din.

Unrequited

She has returned.
I am ecstatic to see her.

Black cat—
Speak to me of freedom.

Her coat is velvet midnight. What
mysteries concealed beneath the inky fur?

I'd like to touch the silky hair but she's lethal. She
stealthily jumps on a blue jay and tears its body open.

Wings and feathers scatter while she eats the rest.
She grows plump but remains sleek and nimble.

Six months without a sign. Who knows where her kind go?
Now she slinks past me and does not once look back to

acknowledge my adoration. When she gets to the compost
at the edge of my yard she shrugs, as if aware I'm watching.

We've encountered each other in this fashion for two
years and a month. She loves her solitude, it's clear.

I love her wildness and hold no intention to make her mine.
She delights and breaks my heart—like one bewitched to

care and worry when she's absent for months—
but never has she cast a glance at me.

The Earth Is Unfinished. So Is Everything

Have I been asleep and it's taken
a squirrel in the woods to wake me up?

It dangles upside down from a tree trunk.
As I approach, it scurries up, jumping
sideways from tree to tree. No brain
damage as it somersaults into the air
and clasps a poplar branch.

I've been told squirrels remember only
10 percent of where they hide nuts. How
nutty. Though the same is said of humans'
brain capacity. The rest, latent, burns or is
buried with us when we die. At least, the
squirrel is skilled in gymnastics. Constantly
views the world differently.

When any creature is knocked dead crossing
the road, how not to think of accidents—
end of a cycle—but time unfolding
with new beginnings? Right now, someone
somewhere is dying. The earth itself is
unfinished. How then, to love this moment,
even this moment—dare to celebrate it.

I'll return home and fall on my knees,
take my beloved's hand, and pledge to stay
as long as I remember where I last left him.

The Ineffable

Again and again, there's a dog. A white German Shepherd, gentle and calm. Tonight, he appeared with an orange tag around his neck. He accompanied me everywhere, yet I don't remember walking out of the house with him. When I looked at my side, he was present. He sat quietly in a chair during class discussions and readings in the seminar room. When the sessions ended, he waited for the students and me to walk out first.

Downstairs, I was briefly alarmed to have left him behind. I turned back, but the stairs were crammed with people. When at last I reached him, still in the chair, a few people—four or five— were stroking him. They asked me his name. I said Joe. He growled a bit and I realized that wasn't his name. I examined his nameless tag and racked my brain, but nothing popped up. I don't know why Joe slipped out of my mouth.

The next day, I smiled at him. It crossed my mind that he was my guide like the dog-headed Anubis, sometimes portrayed in other canine forms attending the scale at the weighing of the heart ceremony or guiding the mummies—escorting souls of ancient Egyptians across the threshold into the afterlife. He had that sort of wisdom about him. His countenance gave the impression that he knew everything.

Later in a dream, I remembered that in my childhood we had a large, white dog called Francisco. The possibility of transmigration filled me with quiet joy.

Acknowledgments

Grateful acknowledgment to the following publications in
which these poems or versions thereof first appeared:

About Place Journal: "Little Wren"

Amethyst Review: "Why I Wake up Early"

Boats Against the Current: "The Dog Is Quiet"

Callaloo: "How Can It Be a Cardinal Sin?" "The Meat-loving God"

Drunk Monkeys: "Don't Bite the Hand That Feeds You"

The Global South: "The Hyena," "Moon Dog"

Hole in the Head Review: "Creation"

Hollins Critic: "Effects of the White Parrot Fairy Tale"

Lady/Liberty/Lit Journal: "The Heart, the Heart, the Hunger"

Mountain Xpress: "Falling in Love"

Prairie Schooner: "Ode to the Sheep"

SWWIM: "Will There Be Chickens in Paradise"

Tiferet Journal: "Locusts"

Tin House: "Factors"

Unbroken Journal: "Between the Dreaming and Becoming"

"City of Antelope" was published in *Capitals: A Poetry Anthology,* ed. Abhay K. (Bloomsbury Publishing, 2017).

"Giant Stag Beetles" was published in *A Literary Field Guide to Southern Appalachia,* eds. Rose McLarney, Laura-Gray Street, and L. L. Gaddy (University of Georgia Press, 2019).

"Factors" was reprinted on poets.org

"Creation" "Falling in Love" "The World is Necessary, Even for Little Ants" were translated into Spanish in *Simpson 7,* trans. Jesús Sepúlveda (Sociedad de Escritores de Chile, 2022).

Immense gratitude to the people, places, and programs that have supported the writing of this book and other creative projects, including Weymouth Center for the Arts & Humanities, The Varda Artists Residency Program, Sylt Foundation African Writers' Residency Award, UNC-Asheville, University of Denver creative writing doctoral program, Syracuse University MFA program, Per Sesh Writing Fellowship, and TrustAfrica.

Special thanks to Diane Lockward for believing in this book and ushering it into the world. All my love to my mentors and guides: Arthur Flowers, Eric Gould, Laird Hunt, Bin Ramke, George Saunders, Goretti Kyomuhendo, Kirk Boyle, Katherine

Zubko, and Michael Burkard. Eternal appreciation for my family and dear friends: Sebastian Matthews, Jeff Davis, Michael Hettich, Jodie Hollander, Jesús Sepúlveda, Casey and Toby King, Amanda Wray, Beverley Nambozo Nsengiyunva, Susan Kiguli, Jackee Batanda, Jennifer McGaha, Christine Boone, Aruni Kashyap, and Adam Fagin.

And deepest thanks to Robert, my faithful reader, insightful adviser, and brilliant soul—the world is lovely with you by my side.

About the Author

Mildred Kiconco Barya is a writer from Uganda now living in North Carolina. Her publications include three earlier poetry books, as well as prose, hybrids, and poems published in *Shenandoah*, *The Cincinnati Review*, *Tin House*, *Prairie Schooner*, and elsewhere. She is a board member of African Writers Trust and Story Parlor. She coordinates the Poetrio Reading events at Malaprop's Independent Bookstore/Café and teaches creative writing and literature at UNC-Asheville. *The Animals of My Earth School* is her fourth full-length poetry collection.

www.mildredbarya.com

CPSIA information can be obtained
at www.ICGtesting.com
Printed in the USA
BVHW042017170323
660681BV00003B/35